Hurt, Healing, and Hope:
Thriving beyond Sexual Assault

Hurt, Healing, and Hope:
Thriving beyond Sexual Assault

A book, performance piece, and journal

Written by Melissa B. Lombardo
Illustrations by Eduardo José Arias Cruz

write
heal
thrive

Copyright Notice

Permissions, Inspiration, and Contributions

The author wishes to acknowledge two written contributions used with permission:
- "And he says to me" by M.R.
- "Remember these things" by Anthony 'Tony' Gali.

Foreword by YWCA New Britain CT Sexual Assault Crisis Service (SACS)

Additionally the author wishes to honor and thank survivors who inspired original content in the monologues, "Hurt", "Training Day", "I Can Sing", and also Take Back the Night Foundation that inspired the monologue, "United We Stand".

Contact

For permission requests, quantity sales, special discounts, production and licensing assistance, speaking engagements, and workshops, contact the author at: info@melissablombardo.com.

Music Use Note

Publisher's Cataloging-in-Publication Data

Hurt, Healing, and Hope: Thriving beyond Sexual Assault

Written by Melissa B. Lombardo. First Edition

1. Creative Non-Fiction - Drama/Performing Arts – Monologues and Scenes

2. Personal Transformation, Sexual Abuse

3. Rape

4. Women

Illustrations by Eduardo José Arias Cruz. *eduardoariascruz.com*

Author portrait by Alicia Ann Daw

Styling by Jessica Dutton

Layout, cover design, and Write, Heal, Thrive logo designed by Nikita Prokhorov. *nikitaprokhorov.com*

Copy editing by Peter J. Lombardo

Printed in the United States of America

Publisher information: Write, Heal, Thrive, West Hartford, CT

ISBN 979-8-9877587-0-0 (paperback)

ISBN 979-8-9877587-1-7 (hardcover)

Library of Congress Cataloging in Publishing Data, Lombardo, Melissa

Library of Congress Control Number: 2023907825

Moving from victims to thrivers is a complex journey, one aided by the reversal of our silence. In "Hurt, Healing, and Hope: Thriving beyond Sexual Assault," Ms. Lombardo returns our voices to us, shaping the way we can hold ourselves in compassion and still reclaim our power. Through her characters' words and discourse, we feel seen, understood, supported, and empowered to acknowledge our pain and carry on. What was once stolen, is now returned: Our hope for the light of a safe, new day.

– Dr. Bridget Cooper, bestselling author of Pain Rebel
& Little Landslides

Melissa Lombardo's Hurt, Healing and Hope: Thriving beyond Sexual Assault" is a brave and powerful piece of writing the world needs now more than ever. As we continue to reckon with justice issues for survivors, part of the problem is that we haven't even been brave or honest enough to tally the total cost. Having had the honor to both read and experience the piece as a performance, in each instance, I was moved forward toward a deeper understanding and felt a sense of what's truly at stake in our healing physically, emotionally, and spiritually.

– Clementina Esposito, The Clementina Collective

Melissa Lombardo's work is an inspirational testament to the ability of survivors of sexual assault to heal by finding their voice to move beyond trauma and how to embrace a brighter, freer future. Whether you are a survivor or support a survivor, this is a MUST READ, pivotal, well-written book and performance piece that can provide a path to health and healing.

– Dorothy Holtermann, Founder of Birth-A-Book, Author, Teacher,
Speaker, Certified Holistic Health Coach

"Your book is ABSOLUTELY needed. SOMEONE needs your book. I am sure of it!"

– Kevin Taylor, Author of Central America: Faces, Places, Food

"The world needs people (like you) to talk about their experiences. I think this is the only way to make a change in this world."

– Dr. Rebeca Sandford Morgan

Melissa Lombardo's Hurt, Healing and Hope: Thriving beyond Sexual Assault is a gift to us all—to those of us who have been sexually abused or assaulted, and to those who have not. For those who have, she speaks directly to our pain, betrayal, confusion and wish to disappear— as well as to our impulses to survive, our need to be believed and understood, and our drive toward healing and hope.

We all know someone who has been sexually assaulted or abused. Melissa's book inspires and invites us to support them and be true allies in the making of a world free of sexual violence.

– Marilyn Cardone, LCSW

"I feel that God has given Melissa healing after her abuse and has shown her a path to move forward in her life. He has also blessed her with the gift of expression so that she can share her experience with others. What a beautiful way to use one's pain: instead of hiding it away, Melissa is telling her story, and those like hers, to impact healing for countless others. This work is truly a gift for anyone to read; to open our eyes, to educate, to bring healing, to give hope."

– K. Leigh Riser

CONTENTS

CONTENTS *(Continued)*

ACT III – Hope • 41

Dedication

To survivors and our healing allies.

To those of you who have been with me on this journey, you know who you are and how you have contributed.

To family and those who have become family.

To Becky, a friend, and inspiration.

To my son.

YWCA New Britain CT Sexual Assault Crisis Service (SACS)

Sexual assault is more than a momentary pain. It is a traumatic event with a lasting impact and can affect nearly every aspect of a survivor's life. Without a support system, survivors of sexual violence are more likely to experience exacerbated trauma symptoms, including fear, guilt, isolation, flashbacks, dissociation, self-harm, or suicidal thoughts. These symptoms can be compounded by increased social and financial burdens of assault such as suffering the loss of friendships or family support, feeling disconnected from a community or a body that has become foreign to the survivor, and losing employment or income. One of the most effective ways to recover the lost sense of self that can accompany a sexual assault is to find a way to reclaim control over the narrative by speaking out.

Melissa Lombardo, author of "Hurt, Healing, and Hope: Thriving beyond Sexual Assault" has found a way to do just that while exploring the diversity of voices and experiences of survivors. Melissa started her journey after connecting with a sexual assault victim advocate post-sexual assault approximately 20 years ago. Working with an advocate planted a seed that led her down an exciting and unexpected path involving world travel, storytelling, advocacy, and self-reflection. This period of healing and recovery allowed her the opportunity to engage with other survivors, learn about the ways sexual violence can impact a life, and use her voice to bring awareness to an experience endured by many but spoken of by very few. Through her work, readers come to appreciate that sexual violence is a crime that does not discriminate based on race, ethnicity, socioeconomic status, gender, age, ability, or sexual orientation. The YWCA New Britain is proud and excited to write the forward for this important work.

The YWCA New Britain Sexual Assault Crisis Service (SACS), a member center of the Connecticut Alliance to End Sexual Violence, offers support services to survivors of sexual violence and their loved ones. At SACS, we strive to honor each individual as they find their own unique and meaningful path toward reclaiming their lives. The core principle of our work is that each survivor is in total control of what happens after an assault. Each person will heal in their own way, in their own time. Our goal is to empower survivors with the information and resources they need to make their own decisions about the care and support they need to begin healing, whether through therapy, activism, volunteering, working with animals, artistic expression, physical fitness, holistic practices, and other methods.

Our advocates are always available through our crisis hotline. We offer to help our survivors navigate the complex systems that they may encounter after experiencing an assault. Depending on each survivor's needs, we find the services that work for them and assist them in creating their own individualized support plan and long-term goals. This may involve finding safe housing, receiving financial assistance to meet their basic needs, working with an attorney to explore legal options, attending support groups, finding long-term mental health services, or simply processing their experiences with their advocate.

Our program is honored and grateful that Melissa has chosen to donate a portion of proceeds from book sales to directly benefit other survivors in our program. These funds make it possible for us to purchase groceries for a survivor who lost their job, an Uber for a survivor who needs to get home from the hospital, a phone for an individual in a domestic violence situation, painting supplies for a survivor support group, and countless other costs associated with keeping survivors safe and supported. We hope this work of art will bring comfort and serve as a catalyst for its readers to continue to find their voice and find healing in their journey.

Sincerely,

YWCA New Britain SACS Team

Content Warning

This is a book and performance piece about rape, sexual assault, and its aftermath. Many people, including me, have suffered sexual violence and trauma and continue to suffer long-term effects.

With so many societal myths about rape, you might be unsure of what constitutes rape. For the purposes of this work, I use the definition of rape as "forced or coerced penetration of any bodily opening using the genitals or other object manipulated by another person" (Kennedy and Hock, 2000, p. 43).

The following pages contain vignettes, short stories, monologues, and details of the hurt and healing resulting from traumatic experiences including rape, sexual assault, domestic violence, and child sexual abuse.

Preface

Our Voices need to be heard.

This "project" began long before it was ever thought of as a project. My experience as a survivor and my love for the written word led me to document a portion of my healing process. Years after the incident, while completing the on-campus phase of my master's degree at the School for International Training (SIT) in Brattleboro, Vermont, I had the opportunity to plan the yearly Sexual Assault Awareness Month (S.A.A.M.) activities. In reviewing pages of experiences from journal entries, I created a collection of interwoven monologues based on my own healing process and experiences around sexual assault. These monologues are presented in "Hurt, Healing, and Hope: Thriving beyond Sexual Assault" previously titled, "Returning to the State of My Body: A Rip in the Veil", which was a first draft vocalized as the final event of S.A.A.M. on the SIT campus in April 2005.

Author Note

The short vignettes of interwoven stories you are about to read or vocalize, bring to life my healing process after sexual assault. If you're a survivor like me, while reading "Hurt, Healing, and Hope" in book form, you may decide to speak the words aloud, giving life to each character as you find your own way through the hurt and into the healing and hope. Prior to beginning this journey of reading or vocalizing, it is beneficial to think about how to process emotions that may arise. Journaling, talking with a friend, or a therapist, or even taking a break from reading is helpful. Healing does not happen right away but as with all new beginnings, this is a start.

As a performance piece, I begin with Act I – Hurt, the traumatic experience(s), then move into Act II – Healing, and finish with Act III – Hope for the future. While my account serves as a basis for the work, experiences inspired by other people and situations are intertwined. It must be said however, that each person is affected by trauma in a different way, and each person's healing process is their own. I have integrated the experiences of others to provide depth and add to the understanding of the relationship between the common threads of rape, sexual assault, child abuse, domestic violence, and healing.

I would not venture to write down my narrative, were it not for my concern and desire for the healing of other survivors and those that support them. It is for these individuals I have created this work, in hope that more silences will be broken, and more healing will begin.

In light and healing,

Characters and Stage Directions

Characters

Each spoken piece reflects the experience of different individuals showing common intersections and the universal trauma of sexual assault. Throughout the work, these four powerful main voices as well as external readers will transmit an array of emotions to the audience.

As a performance piece, this 3–act work can take place in a small intimate theater setting for a cast of (6) Four main characters and two additional outside readers taking a total of 70–80 minutes to perform with an option to hold a post-production discussion to raise awareness of sexual violence and healing.

Each character is dressed in black with a different colored scarf (Teal, Blue, Orange, Yellow) placed on a visible part of their body, i.e., hair, neck, as a sash or as a wrap.

For script purposes, characters are denoted as "ALI" in Teal, "BAE" in Blue, "CHI" in Orange, and "DAE" in Yellow. Names are neither feminine nor masculine. The four characters are telling stories to an audience and sometimes to each other. The stories are sometimes about themselves and sometimes about others. In most cases, the stories are being told directly to the audience.

Two external guest readers may sit in the audience area to speak their parts and/or come onto the stage when it is their turn to read. Wearing black with a different colored scarf is optional for external guest readers.

Stage Direction

There are four bar stools in the middle of a stage at the front of a small theater setting with two additional bar stools off to the side on the stage. An additional bar stool, wide-brim hat, non-working microphone prop and a journal should be placed behind the seat where the character "DAE" will be sitting, for later use. At the start of the production, lights previously directed to the front of the stage are dimmed while the rest of the lights slowly turn off. The only lights at the beginning of the performance are the previously dimmed lights. On the sides and front of the stage there are candles or lanterns that will give the appearance of illuminating the area as the characters enter the stage from the back of the theater.

Four somber, serious individuals enter the stage from the side, and each brings a candle or a lantern as they walk up to the front of the main stage.

A slow almost meditative music plays upon entry to the stage as the characters enter and place the candle or lantern with those previously set up on the stage to give the idea that the four who are entering are bringing additional light to the stage.

The remaining stage lights slowly begin to illuminate while fading up for approximately one minute. Each character places their prop on the stage floor in front of where they will sit and takes a seat on their bar stool.

ACT I
HURT

SOMEONE LIKE US
(Stage Direction: Title read out loud by ALI)

ALI: Who writes about us? Who really writes about us? Who understands us?

BAE: Many would rather live with their heads turned away, eyes closed, looking the other way, glancing at their feet as they pass, most not even knowing what lies within each one of us

CHI: And when some do know, they may only look at us, trying to be consoling, trying to make us laugh, viewing our emotions with such simplicity that makes us angry inside.

DAE: I did not search for this experience any more than I wanted to sleep under a bridge in the cold winter of this country after being raped. No, my search is more than that. My search is real; I look for compassion, for understanding that comes with experience. Maybe that is why so many do not want to acknowledge us unless they are one of us or know someone like us.

SITTING
(Stage Direction: Title read out loud by any character except for ALI with a pause between the title and the start of the dialogue.)

CHI: Sitting alone with no place to go. Listening to the adult conversations from the living room. As a first-born child, she eagerly awaited the prospective sibling. A little baby girl or a little baby boy? Mommy told her she would even be able to help take care of the new baby and that sometimes she would even be able to hold the new baby in her lap.

BAE: Would she hold the new baby the same way he had held her?

CHI: Would she have to touch the new baby where he had touched her?

DAE: No, she would not touch the new baby like that, Daddy made up her mind for her.

CHI: Daddy yelled when he saw the way she was being touched by "that man." She never heard Daddy scream so loud.

BAE: And she never would hear Daddy scream like that again…ever. No one saw "that man" again, and Daddy never even explained why. And the girl now chooses to sit alone.

ALI: I am only four years old and already sitting alone.

SHE ONCE SAT ALONE

BAE: She once sat alone and would continue to sit alone. There was that one time, just when she was coming out of her silence. She was now eight years old. Mom and Dad came home that night and saw her in a daze. The babysitter just smiled and told them she had fallen. He said she was upset but oh, don't worry, she'd be fine, he did a thorough check, a really thorough check.

LYING...SITTING, BUT MANY YEARS LATER

CHI: Does it create a lie to deny your child what they may or may not even remember? How about when that child asks what happened to them so long ago? Does it create a lie to feign disinterest? It squirms in secrecy, and yes, it is creating a lie by not telling them such an important detail of their life, of her life. And so it goes. She is now willingly lying, this time it is horizontal on a bed. He is supposed to love her and try to understand her. This is her first boyfriend, an older "man" to her fifteen years. He is jealous and possessive of her young body. Instead of trying to understand her, he lies next to her, clothes off in a disheveled pile on the floor, hot with frustration, turned away from her. She turns to him to smooth his pain, pushing aside her hurts and finds herself confronting not him but her virginity. She gives up, and her virginity is lost—she is still so young at fifteen years old.

DAE: Does he make all the decisions about what you would do as a couple? Does he usually get his way and not let you assert yourself? Has he ever restricted the people you meet and pressured you into doing something, anything you did not want to do or be?

ALI: Yes, yes, yes (*in a sexually excited way, and then a look of sadness and a sad sigh of defeat*).

CHI: (*facetious, taunting*) Could have been a date rape, could be a rapist...(*spoken normally on this last bit*) and most likely abusive.

HURT

(Back and forth dialogue between ALI and BAE)
(Stage Direction: Title read out loud for emphasis by any character)

ALI: I was hurt.

BAE: I was raped.

ALI: I was badly hurt.

BAE: I was badly raped.

ALI: You cannot see the scars.

BAE: So many years later I cannot even see those scars.

ALI: There were cuts.

BAE: There were cuts down there.

ALI: I saw blood.

BAE: Not a lot, but I saw blood.

ALI: I was hurt.

BAE: I was raped.

ALI: I was badly hurt.

BAE: I was badly raped.

ALI: Raped.

BAE: Cut.

ALI and BAE (*spoken forcefully at the same time*): Scarred.

BACK-AND-FORTH DIALOGUE

(Stage Direction: Alternating between four characters, there is no title to read out loud)

ALI: I was four, twelve, and fifteen.

BAE: I was twenty-one.

CHI: I was six, nineteen, and twenty.

External Guest Reader (*to stand up from a place in the audience*):
         I was fourteen.

DAE: I was five, six and seven and a foster child.

ALI: Mine...pause...by people I knew.

CHI: A family friend, my abusive boyfriend, and my classmate.

External Guest Reader (*to stand up from a place in the audience*):
         An older cousin.

ALI: By a family member, a babysitter, and my boyfriend.

BAE: A classmate on my college campus.

DAE: My stepfather raped me...and then I became a mother.

IT IS NOT YOUR FAULT

(Stage Direction: Title read out loud for emphasis by any character except DAE)

DAE: We were only playing the first time he touched me. "Tickling" he told me and
         asked me if I would tickle him too...

THIS WAS THE MAN...

BAE: This is the man her mother chose to marry after all. She does not want to be the
         cause of yet another of her mother's relationships dissolving. She feels ashamed,
         even embarrassed. She does not want to be home...yet she does not want to be out
         on the streets either. She is fifteen years old. Maybe her mother chose him over

her. Maybe her mother does not even realize that this man is a monster. But her mother is a grown woman. How can she not realize this? Still, she does not want her mother to blame her. Maybe her mother would believe him over her, maybe he would tell her mother that she made the advances on him. He told her by being married to her mother, and she, being her mother's daughter, is an extension of her mother somehow making it possible to continue the abuse. She felt she had no choice, no one to turn to.

CHI: It was finally years later that her mother decided to divorce him, more reason not to say anything; she did not want to make the proceedings worse. She remembered what it was like when her own father walked out on them, the pain, the suffering. She did not want to hurt her mother again. She never told anyone about the late-night telephone calls her now former stepfather made, calling out to her in the dark of night, saying he wanted her and never really wanted her mother.

HOW DO CHILDREN DO IT?

ALI: How do children grow up with sexual abuse around them? Sexual abuse under the covers, in the shower, playing with your favorite bright new red truck on the floor by the kitchen table, alone with "him" when Daddy or Mommy enter the room and do nothing when they see your grandfather touching you in a not-grandfatherly way.

CHI: A poll was taken, an informal poll of grown men in one family who had witnessed all forms of abuse committed by their fathers, grandfathers, uncles, and even brothers. We spoke to these now grown men about traumatic events in their lives. They all had witnessed abuse, both sexual and physical, and there was a common thread between them all.

(Stage Direction: Long Pause between paragraphs)

BAE: *(standing up to speak and then sitting down imitating a lower, gruff voice)*: "Sometimes you just had to focus on the good, to forget, to live, to get by."

External Reader *(standing up to speak and then sitting down)*: "The man that died...he was a good man; he took care of his family."

DAE: *(standing up to speak and then sitting down, imitating a lower baritone voice)*: "I remember summers in the park, we would play ball together, and he took my sister to dances at the local dance hall."

CHI: Yes, all of this said about an abuser, physically, emotionally, and sexually, who even in death seems to control his family...the family who mourns him as if he were a saint, as if he did nothing at all.

CHI: How then do children grow up with abuse?...They pretend.

AND HE TOOK HER
(Stage Direction: Title read out loud for emphasis by any character except DAE)

DAE: And he took her violently from behind...Behind his smirk, he held anger from a place even she did not dare to know. He was not like this when they met, or so she thought. He always treated her with kindness...until they married. Those smiling wedding photos seemed to be from another lifetime, not hers, and not his. His family, his parents...lived the same life. "Us women have got to be strong," her mother-in-law once told her. Both were beaten when she unknowingly and innocently repeated this to her husband. And now, here she was, her husband taking advantage of their sacred marriage vows, the kids in the other room pretending not to know their father's intent, and he, becoming angrier for her lack of emotion, angry at her willingness to let him take her so easily and so violently from behind.

SHE WAS RAPED

CHI: She was raped.

ALI: Having his baby at the age of eighteen.

BAE: She was raped.

ALI: By someone she knew.

BAE: She was raped.

CHI: She never trusted him. And now she is lying flat on a table in this guy's kitchen.

ALI: A child is raped and produces a child.

BAE: A child is given up to an adoption agency.

ALI: Neither can take care of themselves.

BAE: She was raped.

All characters: We were raped.

DO THINGS REALLY HAPPEN IN THREES?
(Stage Direction: Title read out loud by ALI, CHI to read entire vignette)

CHI: Three times, three different places and three different faces. My mother always said that things happen in threes.

　　　　Molested when I was maybe six, not remembering a lot, only remembering what my parents told me. Many years later at the age of nineteen, an abusive boyfriend completely took advantage of me. I had to run away to a friend's house and hide my car so he could not find me. I was terrified he was going to enter the house and try to take me hostage. I remember the phone call, the drive-bys, and the way he would show up at my apartment and sit outside waiting for me. I was so scared.

The third time—things that happen in threes will come to an end.

I was house-sitting for a foreign friend while he returned to his home country. I was away from my familiar surroundings in an isolated area of town. I always had friends, but after this experience, I was different. I did not want to see anyone. I was someone else.

The perpetrator was someone that I knew. A former classmate. We left at the same time, from the same building, there was an upcoming exam, we agreed to meet up and study. Afterwards we had dinner and he would not leave until he got his dessert. When it was finally over, he left, and I could not tell anyone. He had threatened me. I did not want to talk about it nor think about it. I did not want anyone to know. I wanted to pretend it didn't happen and I wanted to die.

I have been living like that for a long time. I have tried to block out my past the best I could and start anew.

My family does not know, none of my friends...neither do you. Look around this room. Come on, look around. You know what? You can look around all you want, and you will never find me. I might be the person who sits next to you in class or on the bus. I might laugh out loud at a joke you make, you might even have been one of my boyfriends. But you will never know, for I have become a statistic, a nameless and faceless statistic.

MY FAULT
(Stage Direction: read title out loud except for BAE)

BAE: It's your fault, he said to me, after what felt like my "confession" to him, like a priest on Judgment Day condemning me to my own personal H*ll.

ALI: Your fault? He really said it was your fault?!

BAE: Yeah, he told me it was my fault. The love of my life telling me it was my fault. Yeah, you know, it was the old "blame the victim" story line. And when I asked him what he meant by that, he blamed me, "Yeah, your fault, you know, you let him into your home. You knew this guy, and you even invited him into your home, and you had dinner with him."

CHI: But that was after you kindly rejected his offer to eat at his home, get into his car, and go to his neighborhood.

ALI: And that was all done in the name of safety.

BAE: Apparently that was not enough. And tell that to the love of your life, the first relationship you were able to have after that fateful evening when the course of your life changed, who is supposed to support you, but now has misplaced his common sense and doesn't even speak the same language. He even went so far as to say, "Still you DID it, and it was YOUR choice!"

DAE: Yeah, to study, to have dinner, not forced sex, not rape! To which he replied, "Well, maybe, then, just maybe it was not your fault."

Spoken together by all characters except for Ali *(emphasis growing with each repetition)*:
         Maybe?!...Maybe?!...Maybe?!

BAE: Exactly, and that is when I took up running away. Running away was the story of my life for so many years.

MY BODY

BAE: Stiff, unfeeling.

         Too much taken onto it.

         I let myself take too much.

         Out of pity, and self-degradation.

         Letting my body be taken advantage of.

         Not feeding my own needs.

         Catering to Them.

         A realm of life that inhabits me, inhibits me, prohibits, and abuses me.

TRAINING DAY
(Stage Direction: Title read out loud by ALI)

CHI: It was one time, one horrible time. An acquaintance used force and intimidation to achieve a means to his end.

DAE: It was one time at a fast-food restaurant, on her first day of training.

CHI: That was then, this is now.

DAE: He gave her a fountain drink with a date rape pill, took her to his house, raped her.

BAE: It was more than one time. My best friend was sexually abused by her uncle from a young age. Her mother died. She lived with her addict father and his brother. She was removed from her home and put into foster care.

CHI: He is in my past. I have learned so much since then. He and his memory leave an imprint, he may be a part of my past, he is not in any way MY PAST.

BAE: Neglect, sexual abuse, undernourishment, she was too young to know what was happening.

DAE: It took her time to realize what had occurred. She dreamt of shadowy darkness and blurry images. Nightmares plagued her sleep.

BAE: It happened to her older sister who lived her life in a wheelchair. She finally decided to speak out. They both testified at their uncle's trial. Horrific events vocalized before a grand jury, a conviction, and a sentence.

CHI: The experience makes up a long list of experiences all of which I learn from.

DAE: We celebrate the end of the nightmares and the beginning of her future.

CHI: I live NOW, I do not live THEN.

I live in the present, not the past.

I move forward into the future although I cannot help but look back.

I rule my life, not him.

The time is now. I will continue.

END ACT I

ACT II
HEALING

UNITED WE STAND

(Stage Direction: Read title out loud for emphasis by any character)

BAE: Rape, what does it mean to you?...Sexual assault? Oh, how about that one? Does it evoke an image, a face, many faces, known, unknown, old, young, girls, boys, men, and women? How about wives, girlfriends, boyfriends, husbands, classmates, your sister, your mother, your uncle, and even you or your father? Rape and sexual assault are color-blind, people blind.

ALI: Every 73 seconds another "U.S. American" is sexually assaulted. Of those, 8 out of 10 rapes are committed by a person known to their victim. Over fifty percent of all rapes occur in the victim's home. Did you know that one in six North American women and one in thirty-three North American men will become victims of rape in their lifetime and transgender students and students of color are at a higher risk for sexual violence? Rape is a crime motivated by a need to control, humiliate, and inflict harm.

All Characters *(shouting):* ALL PEOPLE Unite! Tonight is our night!

(Stage Direction: Medium Pause)

DAE: *(shouting):* What do we want?

All Characters: *(shouting):* No more Sexual Assault!

DAE: *(shouting):* When do we want it?

All Characters Together: NOW! No means NO and Yes means YES. Sexual Assault is against the law!

MY BODY SHOULD BE

BAE: My body should be my temple, a place of comfort, to reflect and think about my life and myself.

CHI: My body, respected by me and everyone in contact with me.

DAE: Intimacy and my feelings on how I view my body are related. If I do not have positive feelings for my body, how can I become intimate with other people in any way, shape, or form?

ALI: I am not intimate and involved with my own feelings concerning my body. If I am uncomfortable with my body, and therefore myself, how can others feel comfortable with me if I am not comfortable with myself?

All Characters: How can we accept others so well and not accept ourselves?

ALI: We must work towards the most important form of acceptance: Self-acceptance.

LA CLINICA - LOSING INNOCENCE

(Stage Direction: Title read out loud by ALI
and most of vignette read by ALI with one intervention from BAE)

ALI: La Clinica—The Clinic. I didn't think too much about it, that I would ever end up here. So now, here I am, in a small, unassuming house that knew me as number three–fifty–five. This is a place of hope and a place of heartbreak. I never thought I would be tested like this, tested for AIDS, Chlamydia, and a whole bunch of other diseases. In fact, sitting here I feel like I am a walking disease. How irrational of me to think that an STD would not even become a possibility. Now here I am losing my pride to try to regain my dignity. I think about it once more as I sit there on a torn plastic cushioned chair and still, I am not sure why I never thought of this before. Anyway, it doesn't even matter; here I am "en Una Clinica"—in a Clinic. For only five dollars I will know my future. The rest of my life now depends on five dollars.

BAE: It is kind of like the lottery. You know, from an individual standpoint or some study, La Clinica is kind of like playing a slot machine. We pay our money and receive our fate. We either come out positive or negative. Why I am here will soon be met with nothing more than an answer of: "Yes, you have it," or "No, you don't."

(Stage Direction: Vignette continued by ALI)

ALI: There were two men waiting in the room ahead of me. The older one was talking to the younger, who was waiting for someone. "We have to be careful of the women," said one. "But the women have to be careful of us, too," replied the other.

"Next, number three–fifty–three," shouted out the woman in red behind the counter without even looking up.

"It'll be alright, man," said the older to the younger "Don't you worry now."

Then the older one looked at me and said he wanted to, "share me a poem." Then suddenly, "Don't worry; I will not try to pick you up." To which I replied, "I figured just as much, we are in an STD clinic, after all" and we both laughed at the thought.

ALIENATION

(Stage Direction: Read title out loud for emphasis by any character)

CHI: And there she was, alienated in her own body, again, for the thousandth time again.

Why, why did she not feel at home there in her body? Where was her essence? Was she even human anymore?

She shivered to herself, constantly searching for sex to forget, blocking out the images of the rape, the abuse, of all that made her dirty. Creating a hollow shell of the individual that once existed. Yes, there she was, alienated, hurting, not sure where to go next, not even being able to be *(short pause, places a hand on heart)*...here.

THE MOTHER IN ME
(Stage Direction: Stand and gently pick up the blanket on the extra stool and have character roll it up into a form that mimics the form of a bundled infant as they walk to the front of the stage)

DAE: The mother in me wants to protect the boy in you. The boy that was forced to watch his female cousin changing her clothes, the boy that was forced to sit on top of her or have her on top of him. All those suggestive movements in the name of a "game." It is only now you are seeing it as abuse. You were eight, nine, and ten years back then. You tried to tell someone who said that you were lying and that you should, "toughen up" and, "not be such a sissy". Abuse can happen to anyone as it happened to you.

BE A HERO, RECOGNIZE THE ABUSE
(Stage Direction: The bundled infant blanket from the previous vignette turns into a superhero cape tied loosely around the characters neck. Title read out loud for emphasis by any character except DAE. Once this piece is read, DAE returns to their seat and removes their cape.)

DAE: I ask you, how are you going to recognize the abuse of a son, a daughter, a sister, or a nephew? It is difficult, but the last thing you need to do is stop believing it isn't there. Although the abuser might be an uncle, a stepfather, or a teacher, never stop believing your child. Many times, you might want to look for other reasons for a change in behavior...always keep the possibility open that your child is being abused. Talk about sexual abuse at an early age, ask your children, get involved in their lives, and look for changes and never, NEVER not believe them when they tell you they are being abused. Ask questions, get more information from them. Do not dismiss and walk away. Give them your full attention. *(Dae returns to stool)*.

IT HAPPENED TO ME
(Stage Direction: Title read out loud by BAE)

ALI: Anything.

CHI: Can happen, may happen.

DAE: Even if you do not want it to happen.

BAE   *(Dramatically yells out)*: DON'T let the past bar you from the present. One awful experience does not mean that all future experiences will be awful.

All Characters except BAE (*hushed or whisper*):

Hard to say, harder to believe.

HEALING
(for Anshul)
(Stage Direction: Title read out loud by Ali)

DAE: They did not know they saved her in the process of saving another...

BAE: You saved a girl one day at your college from being raped that fateful night in the dormitory in one of the many college campuses in the world.

DAE: Whatever was going to happen did not because of you.

CHI: "But I wish I was there to help you; I wish I was there to do something."

CHI: "You did not deserve for this to happen, my G*D, why did this have to happen to you?!"

ALI: "But don't you see? You were there to save me, you did help me, you did something, because when you saved her in the past, you rescued me in the future. Because of people like you, my healing continues."

AND HE SAYS TO ME
(Stage Direction: Title read out loud by ALI. 1st External Guest Reader to read vignette. Guest reader will stand up and enter the stage with a candle or lantern, place it in front of their bar stool and sit down prior to reading. At the end of the reading, the guest reader remains sitting.)

External guest reader: First. Know that I love you and I am not the only one who loves you. You made a conscious decision to transcend your traumatic experiences and made some difficult, brave, and necessary choices. You've always fought against injustice but fighting for yourself is something you've had to learn. I'm proud of you for doing so well, though I never doubted that you would.

REMEMBER THESE THINGS
(Stage Direction: Title and vignette to be read by 2nd External Guest Reader. Guest reader will stand up and enter the stage with a candle or lantern, place it in front of their bar stool and sit down prior to reading. At the end of reading, the guest reader remains sitting.)

External guest reader: You are special, and the world needs you.

Everything you do is useful.

Stick close to those who are kind. They allow you to show that you are kind as well.

If all else fails, beat the crap out of a punching bag and scream into a pillow...
(Short pause)

YOU

(Stage Direction: Read title out loud for emphasis by any character)

ALI: You...

BAE: Cried for me, with me, within me.

ALI: ...You.

CHI: I.

BAE: Spoke my heart as you spoke your own.

CHI: I

BAE: Listened to your unspoken words.

All Characters: We.

BAE: Shared healing.

All Characters: We.

BAE: Shared life.

All Characters: We.

...Are

...One.

BAE: Until we meet again, smile for me. Do not cry for me.

END ACT II

ACT III
HOPE

YOUR EYES

(Stage Direction: Title read out loud for emphasis. ALI should stand up with a journal to read and look towards the audience for this piece.)

ALI: I found what I was looking for…in your eyes.

By looking into your eyes, I feel renewed faith.

Eyes that hold trust and love, honesty and respect.

I had almost given up.

Everything I stopped searching for,

I see in the depths of your eyes.

I found a part of what I was looking for…in your eyes.

Unknowingly, this moment has been worth the wait.

(Stage Direction: Short Pause before continuing)

BAE: My healing has been like wet rocks after the rain.

Freshness that washed away the dirt,

Cleansing the gold of heaven that lay among the rubble,

Giving life another chance!

Rebirth of a new silver lining in a rejuvenated waters' stream.

(Stage Direction: Pause before continuing)

CHI: For a long while I stopped feeling, and little by little, I have allowed myself to feel again. The small details matter most, and I cherish those moments, these moments…and now, I can dance again…I can dance!

IT WAS A MONDAY

(Stage Direction: Title read out loud by ALI)

CHI: Today I lived, I really lived. It's the start of the week and the end of my hibernation from dancing.

ALI: I danced; I took a step, just one, but that one step will become two, and then three. One step that will last longer than these ten seconds.

CHI: I shed a layer today and moved forward.

ALI: I did it and it felt uncomfortable. I did it, I got through it, and it was OKAY, more than okay, it was incredible, so much progress made by that one dance step, I feel bigger than life itself.

ALI: I shout for joy and hear it reverberating on a pond of musical integrity.

Do I lack movement? Do I lack the vitality for life I once had? You don't get to decide...I just did!

MAYBE WE CAN DANCE
(for I.O.)
(Stage Direction: Title read out loud for emphasis by any character.
Play a few beginning bars of a guitar upbeat tune prior to reading)

BAE: The air is fresh, I can breathe.

Just like after a good yoga class, the blood is flowing freely through my body.

Sitting, in silence.

Outside, alone, and now you enter.

I don't ruin the moment.

And without much thought, I think, "maybe we can dance!"

WITH ALL THIS BEING SAID
(Stage Direction: Title read out loud for emphasis by DAE reading out of a journal)

DAE: I own my life. I make good, caring choices for my life.

I will live my life the way that will help me grow.

With the people who will help me grow.

I will keep out those people who do not deserve to be in my life.

I will keep anything out of my life that will not help me grow.

I own my life.

I deserve everything beautiful.

I am taking back control of my body and my life.

HOME
(Stage Direction: Title read out loud for emphasis by any character)

ALI: I have finally found my way.

CHI: Home is a feeling; home is much more than a place, I am home in my body, I am at home in my soul.

DAE: I am my decisions.

ALI: I am my accomplishments.

BAE: Looking back, I never realized to what extent my disassociation would so drastically change my coming back through healing. Each new day led me to a place that I could not even comprehend. I frequently asked: Where would all this lead? I felt so small in such a big world.

RETURNING TO THE STATE OF MY BODY!

(Stage Direction: Title read out loud by ALI) *This is an interviewer and an interviewee format for a talk show. DAE speaks the entire piece as two characters (one as an interviewer and another as the interviewee), standing and changing position in the front of the audience as DAE switches between "characters." DAE should be "facing" "each other" as a host and guest would do. DAE should use a prop such as a hat and a microphone to denote when it is the interviewer and when it is the interviewee. DAE can also take the extra 5th bar stool that is behind them on the stage and place that stool along with the stool they have been sitting on during the production to the front of the stage. The character may also read this vignette standing up and switching characters between Dae the interviewer and Dae the interviewee. There is a certain emphasis placed on the words "My Body" as this is the name of the state being referred to.)

DAE as Interviewer:

Hello and good morning, and what a morning it is. Welcome to our program, "Returning to the State of My Body." We are here today talking with our special guest, Me. Welcome to our show, Me.

DAE interviewee:

Thank you, thank you; it is a pleasure to be here, not only here on your program, but in the "State of My Body."

DAE as interviewer:

Me, so that everyone knows, can you explain to us a little about where you went and what you have done for the past four years when we could not find you?

DAE interviewee:

Of course. Over the last four years I left the "State of My Body" in search of something. It was, let me tell you, it was an experience that pushed me outside the trauma, outside of memories, and without knowing what else to do, or that I was leaving at all, I left, yes, I left the most precious state in the world for a place very protected and safe, but also joyless and lifeless...until that fateful day, the day that I returned...

DAE as interviewer:

What you are sharing with me, is incredible because it must have been so hard to return. What we really want to know is how you returned, and what happened to make you change your mind and come back. Can you tell us about that?

DAE interviewee:

Dear friends, family, and acquaintances, when I left, I lost the happiness and will to live, and even waking up each morning and going through the routine of a day became the most difficult. In the four years I was gone, I lived away from the center of the state of my body. But even throughout, there were changes, small ones, the evening I was able to get into a taxi with a stranger, the day I did not wake up crying, the moment I was able to begin taking care of myself without being prodded by others, the time I smiled, and it was real. One day I realized the changes would not stop and I would have to reenter the state I left so many years ago. Well, that gave me such a terrible fright, but in the end, I tentatively jumped on the first sun beam and began the journey back to my heart, the capital of the "State of My Body." Finally, step by step, I continued to move forward using various methods of soul-searching transportation, and I took what each had to offer, and as you see me now, here I am.

DAE as interviewer:

What you are sharing is amazing.

DAE interviewee:

Thank you. Each day is a step. I learned something in those four years, I learned that things are not always so great, but with the strength to return, what you gain in the end is the best gift in the world. Returning to the "State of My Body" leaves me without words. Believe me when I say I felt wonderful, filled with life, and happy when I finally returned. It is exactly so, and to see the result of so much work. I have encountered the greatest reward, the journey in searching for the rainbow, the "State of My Body." Healing is just that. It is this and more, and I am so happy.

DAE as interviewer:

Thank you, and welcome back.

DAE interviewee:

You are welcome, I am so happy to be here with all my supporters.

(Stage Direction: Short Pause)

DAE as interviewer:

Now let us listen to some of our favorite tunes as we return to regularly scheduled programming...*(Long Pause)*

DAE as interviewer:

Yes, a few songs and an introduction by a thriver who found her voice during the healing process...

I CAN SING

BAE: In the beginning, there I was, an innocent little "vagina" protected only by a pair of white cotton underwear that my mother bought me. I wore these from the day I left diapers until the day I discovered sexy lingerie. It was then, at the age of fifteen, that I left granny underwear behind in hopes of finding greener pastures. There was this one fateful day that led me to believe that greener pastures only exist in fairy tales. No, it wasn't the start of my period, which scared me half to death. No, the day I am talking about is the day I was "discovered" by others, or more particularly, one "other," who really did not care what underwear I was wearing, or how great I smelled after a nice washing. Nope, I tell you, it did not matter that I grew my hair out so fine and became a mature vagina. Heck, that dick wouldn't have cared anyway.

After that day I decided to cut my hair, not bathe, and basically forget I existed.

This couldn't go on forever, though the granny starch white cotton underwear was always readily available.

Hmm, little by little, I decided to grow my hair out again, a symbolic awakening, if you ask me, though you might find that sort of thing kind of odd.

Now, years later, I've taken up singing lessons. Yes, *(short pause)* me, someone who wouldn't even...sing in the shower with imposter syndrome in the big world now sings. Go ahead, laugh all you want, just you wait and see, and then it will be you asking to hire me for your next event.

BAE continues. *(Sing the following invented lyrics in any style)*:

Never knew how much I loved me, I never knew how much I cared. Every time I take a step forward it's a feeling that I love to feel, I give me healing...*(singing trails off)*

See, I told you, I can sing, and you know what, now it is my turn to let you in on a little secret, move over beautiful people here I come. Those that came before me inspired me to speak out. As time went on I decided it was time for me to start singing about....*(pause)*...us, the healers, the thrivers. Let me share a few of the songs with you just so you can sing out loud in the years to come...

ALI: Let's go now...

BAE: Come on everyone.

ALI: Do you believe in yourself...because I've got something to say about it. It goes a little like this...

(Both BAE and ALI. Sing the following invented lyrics):

Don't go for second best,

Be yourself and put that to the test.

You know, you know, you've got to.

Help yourself express how you feel.

And then become the shining star that's real

BAE: and,...

(Both BAE and ALI. Sing the following invented lyrics):

"We Just Wanna Heal and Have Fun, oh yeah, yeah, yeah, we are going to heal and have fun".

So, how do you like that, see, I told you. Once I was able to begin healing I felt my whole world open up and I know the same can happen to you. Hey, and one more thing, if you want to sign up for singing lessons, I'll be over there after the show.

BAE: *(Points to back of room)*.

FORGIVING MYSELF
(Stage Direction: Title read out loud by ALI)

CHI: How can I forgive myself and move forward?

Like there is any other way. I must move forward and continue healing for my own inner peace and future.

No one controls my life except myself.

They do not control me.

I must be compassionate with my younger self.

I forgive me for the pain I carried within for so long

I move forward.

I am beautiful.

ALI: I was quiet, or so I perceived myself, and sometimes still do.

As a girl I was not as assertive as I am now. As a woman I have grown into my body.

I have developed boundaries, broken barriers, spoken my mind, and continue to do so. I trust my instincts more than ever; looking for goodness, knowing not all is good and being okay with that.

DAE: I have come a long way and still have a way to go. I have accomplished a lot, and now as a woman it is more purposeful. I am learning and beginning to achieve new balance.

BAE: I am a woman now, and it is up to me to recognize beauty in my life and in myself.

I did not want to feel, to feel was to acknowledge and to acknowledge was to face the pain. Feeling meant confronting. It means recognizing a very hurtful initiation into womanhood. If this was a woman's initiation, then I wanted nothing to do with it. Womanhood was not for me...for a very, very long time, it was not for me.

WOMANHOOD

(Stage Direction: Title read out loud by ALI. ALI to read the vignette after pausing)

When did womanhood become for me? Was it the day I finally wore a skirt? Was it when I danced the night away at "Café Nuit"? Maybe it was the day I told my siblings that I was abused. Or the day I said yes to a date? Was it the first time I had sex and did not cry? Or the first time I consciously denied sex and did not get hurt? Maybe womanhood is more than those things and yet maybe it is all those things. There were great moments in this womanhood's healing cycle; the day of the short skirt was amazing. I put on the skirt in the morning, ate breakfast, opened the front door of my house and walked outside. I walked down the street and saw regular people like you and me. Some looked up at me and others just kept going about their regular everyday lives. I felt so out of place in the skirt and returned home. I changed back into my long pants. It was an incredible moment. I now had a choice, pants, or a skirt. In the end I realized that womanhood for me was making these choices. I never really lost my womanhood in the aftermath of the rape. I just decided to hide my womanhood from those "manhoods" out there. I chose to hide my womanhood until I was able to grow into my new role as a woman, a woman passing through a painful initiation. I became a woman; stronger by recognizing my journey and with the support of an eclectic and often ironic community of individuals. A woman's journey, a man's journey, a person's journey is validated by those around them and their journey after trauma is only possible with the support of others who help guide them to their own unique healing process.

REMEMBERING

(Stage Direction: Title read out loud for emphasis by any character except CHI)

CHI: The road unseen lies close ahead.

Unknowing where the road will lead.

Not recognizing the journey until the end.

Nervous and worried.

Frightened of what might be.

Opening that door anyway.

What comes next is the most frightening.

A door closes as you move forward on the path.

Turning to look back, but unable to return unless you continue.

Taking small steps to the new destination.

Staying on the path is a task.

Every step you take advances, even if you take a step backwards or retract, it is important to start again and continue moving forward.

Moving ahead may feel like wandering in the dark and searching for a light.

Inevitable changes and challenges bring uncertainties in the healing process after rape.

Time heals and at some point, you begin to live.

YOU ARE HERE
(Stage Direction: Title read out loud by ALI. ALI to read the vignette)

ALI: The moment is now; this is the reward for living. It does not matter how you got here, only that you are here and need to start walking. Wherever you are going is just as important as what you do when you get there. Right now, you are here; it is what comes next, where you go. That is entirely up to you. I woke up one day, and it was a breezy, sunny afternoon. My feet suddenly began walking. How did I get here, where am I heading? The sky was bright, my feelings were low. But all seems good on a breezy afternoon. There is nothing in life that is too big or cumbersome to handle. Finally, the clouds are lifting over my head. I put on my jacket and start to walk to the dock, to the pond, to the next parking lot, walking my troubles away into the next new day and celebrating each little advance, each moment, every step, being grateful and finding joy in the journey.

LIFE DOES NOT SCARE ME
(Stage Direction: Title read out loud for emphasis by any character except BAE)

BAE: I sit here now four years later seeking out the answers to the past and waiting expectantly for the future, each day in the making.

I have traveled abroad and learned a new language.

I am not scared of what comes next.

Sunsets have risen hundreds of times witnessed by my very eyes.

Life does not scare me.

Thousands more suns will set in time.

Where will I be? I do not know.

This does not even scare me.

Up on a mountaintop.

Down by a river.

Life is good.

Life does not scare me!

DAE: I am going home...with the support of my friends, my family, my community, mi Corazon, my heart. It is the place I call home. Life brought me to this place, the safeness that I have found, right here, right now, and that I will take and carry with me, as a special intention, a positive thought, the feeling of love.

(Stage Direction: Slow Fade out of lights so that the entire stage is illuminated. Cue music, something light, hopeful, upbeat)

END OF ACT III

My journey to publishing has been a long one. Initially, this work was written as journal entries while I was an undergraduate student trying to piece together the sequence of events of my past. During graduate school, I transformed the entries into interwoven spoken monologues. Many years later, I "mentored" my younger self, to continue my healing process, revisit the monologues, gain new insight, and now take the next step to publish. Never again do I want to let my voice go unheard. In revisiting "Hurt, Healing, and Hope: Thriving beyond Sexual Assault" 20 years later, it is my hope that we continue to find and use our voices and break more silence.

In continued healing,

Due to the sensitivity of this topic, emotions may arise after reading or vocalizing this work and you may be unsure how to handle them. Reaching out for support can help. You may choose a trusted person to talk to or you can contact your local 24-hour Crisis Center for immediate assistance. Help is always available. I encourage you to reach out when you need support.

The YWCA New Britain Connecticut Sexual Assault Crisis Service (SACS): 1-888-999-5545 offers bilingual English-Spanish assistance to sexual assault survivors and their loved ones throughout the state of Connecticut.

The Rape, Abuse, and Incest National Network (R.A.I.N.N.) operates a confidential National Sexual Assault Hotline in the United States of America. You can call 24 hours a day: 1-800-656-HOPE.

Post-reading Discussion

Conversing with others is a good way to process topics such as sexual assault and sexual violence as is self-reflection. You may want to respond to the below questions either by yourself or with others and use the accompanying blank pages to take notes.

1. There are many different types of sexual assault. What examples come to mind?

2. What are some of the myths surrounding sexual violence?

3. Many incidents of sexual violence go unreported. Why might a survivor of sexual violence not report it?

4. Have you ever had a hard time speaking up? Describe the scenario. How did you feel? How did you find your voice?

5. What coping mechanisms do you use when going through a difficult time?

6. In what ways can you support a survivor in their journey to healing?

7. Self-care is very important for both survivors and their support system. What can you do to incorporate self-care into your life?

8. Please add your own reflection question here:

_____

_____

_____

_____

_____

_____

_____

_____

I would love to hear your unique reflection questions or your responses to the above questions. All responses will remain confidential .

You may share with me at: info@melissablombardo.com.

Book Discussion Reflection Responses *(Continued)*

_____

_____

_____

_____

_____

_____

_____

_____

_____

_____

_____

_____

_____

_____

_____

_____

_____

_____

_____

_____

_____

_____

_____

_____

_____

_____

_____

_____

_____

_____

_____

_____

_____

_____

_____

_____

_____

_____

_____

_____

_____

_____

_____

_____

_____

_____

_____

_____

_____

_____

_____

_____

_____

Book Discussion Reflection Responses *(Continued)*

_____

_____

_____

_____

_____

_____

_____

_____

_____

_____

_____

_____

_____

_____

_____

_____

_____

_____

_____

_____

_____

_____

_____

_____

_____

_____

_____

Journaling - Write, Heal, Thrive

Journaling can be a powerful tool. Recommended by mental health professionals, journaling can help you organize your thoughts for self-reflection, help release mental blocks, and reduce stress and anxiety. For me, journaling has many benefits including writing as healing and a path to thriving.

In the following section of this book, you will find blank pages to journal thoughts, and feelings, or write your own monologues of Hurt, Healing, and Hope. Since healing is never linear, you may use the following pages to write in any way that feels right to you and only if you feel comfortable doing so. I trust that you know more about what you need than I do. You may choose to write, doodle, or share any thoughts you may have, whether it be part of your own story or words of encouragement for someone else. This is your personalized journal and your voice matters. You are on a path to healing, and I commend you as you start this courageous and challenging journey.

It is my hope that writing may assist you in manifesting greater healing.

In healing and thriving,

_____

_____

_____

_____

_____

_____

_____

_____

_____

_____

_____

_____

_____

_____

_____

_____

_____

_____

_____

_____

_____

_____

_____

_____

_____

_____

_____

_____

_____

_____

_____

_____

_____

_____

_____

_____

_____

_____

_____

_____

_____

_____

_____

_____

_____

_____

_____

_____

_____

_____

_____

_____

_____

_____

_____

_____

_____

_____

_____

_____

_____

_____

_____

_____

_____

_____

_____

_____

_____

_____

_____

_____

_____

_____

_____

_____

_____

_____

_____

_____

_____

_____

_____

_____

_____

_____

_____

_____

_____

_____

_____

_____

_____

_____

_____

_____

_____

_____

_____

_____

_____

_____

_____

_____

_____

_____

_____

_____

_____

Write, Heal, Thrive *(Continued)*

_____

_____

_____

_____

_____

_____

_____

_____

_____

_____

_____

_____

_____

_____

_____

_____

_____

_____

_____

_____

_____

_____

_____

_____

_____

_____

_____

_____

_____

_____

_____

_____

_____

_____

_____

_____

_____

_____

_____

_____

_____

_____

_____

_____

_____

_____

_____

_____

_____

_____

_____

_____

_____

_____

_____

_____

_____

_____

_____

_____

_____

_____

_____

_____

_____

_____

_____

_____

_____

_____

_____

_____

_____

_____

_____

_____

_____

_____

Write, Heal, Thrive *(Continued)*

_____

_____

_____

_____

_____

_____

_____

_____

_____

_____

_____

_____

_____

_____

_____

_____

_____

_____

_____

_____

_____

_____

_____

_____

_____

_____

_____

_____

_____

_____

_____

_____

_____

_____

_____

_____

_____

_____

_____

_____

_____

_____

_____

_____

_____

_____

_____

_____

_____

_____

_____

_____

_____

_____

_____

_____

_____

_____

_____

_____

_____

_____

_____

_____

_____

_____

_____

_____

_____

_____

_____

_____

_____

_____

_____

_____

_____

_____

_____

_____

_____

_____

_____

_____

_____

_____

_____

_____

_____

_____

_____

_____

_____

_____

_____

_____

_____

_____

_____

_____

_____

_____

_____

_____

_____

_____

_____

_____

_____

_____

_____

_____

_____

_____

Acknowledgments

This book and performance piece would not be in your hands if it were not for the encouragement and support of many people including survivors who have shared their stories giving me the courage to continue my journey. I would like to thank the following individuals and organizations that contributed to my healing process and, by extension, this project. Sarvelia Peralta-Duran and Ryland White, Sissi Loftin, Beatriz Fantini, of the SIT Center for Intercultural Programs (CIP) and Diversity Office, members and volunteers of the SIT Sexual Assault and Violence Educators (Project S.A.V.E). Valuable support came from Reed Colver, stage director, editor, and friend; the ladies and gentlemen from the Bolton Dormitory; Protasia Gathendoh, Chrissy Hyde, Dennis Winkler, and Jessica Marchese. I am grateful to my first readers: Cyndi Cain-Fitzgerald, Reed Colver, Peter Dillon, Deniece Dortch, Christopher Forbrook, Reagan Jackson, Carolyn Little, Sira Perez, Jaimena Shah, Ryland White, Kathy Wohlfeld, and others who collectively gave a voice to every survivor. I am grateful to individuals and organizations including singer and songwriter Gina Forsyth and her song, "You Are Here", Judith Reichsman and Interplay of Vermont, Mary Ertel and her community drum circle in Vernon, CT., the YWCA New Britain Connecticut Sexual Assault Crisis Services (SACS) and my first counselor who encouraged me to journal.

This work would not have been possible if not for my partner, the very talented illustrator, and ever-patient Eduardo José Arias Cruz, who has been by my side for more moments than I can count, Nikita Prokhorov, a life-long friend, confidant, and talented graphic designer and lettering artist, and my brother Peter J. Lombardo, who worked tirelessly to edit and proofread many drafts of this manuscript.

I am grateful for Sobeyda Alvarez-Inestroza, a friend and SIT colleague who worked with me to create a Spanish translation of this book and performance piece. Because of her, I can bring Hurt, Healing, and Hope to a broader audience. I am also thankful for Ernesto "Tito" Davila, Annabella Gini Lombardo, Maria Margarita Miranda Diaz, and Andrés Arias Lombardo. They provided key translation and proofreading support in Spanish during various stages of this project.

To my early pre-publishing community, authors: Dr. Bridget Cooper, Elizabeth (Beth) Bolton, Dr. Christopher Minio,

Olivia Ballinger, Jimmy LeSage, Dana Remedios, Nzima Hutchings, Kristina Hiller, Roger Alfredo Martinez also known as el Psicologo Martinez, Patrina Dixon, Clementina Esposito, Dorothy Holtermann, and the "Birth-a-Book" writing group, your contributions in my life are immeasurable and you have each inspired me to continue moving forward. Other writers and online publishing communities have also been integral in my next steps in the journey, as has my sister Michelle, who has lent her voice to a live version of the monologues.

To Guayo, Andrés, LaLa, my parents Janice and Peter, my siblings Michelle Helen and Peter J., my mother-in-law Anita Cruz, Leigh Riser; and her "tapestry of ideas" and editing support, M.R; for being the first person I spoke to after many months of silence, and to Alvaro Berroteran, Dan Lester, Ana Paula Benitez, Anthony (Tony) Gali, Kate Morgan, César Andino, Josephine Eichler, Maureen Cody Carroll, Tania Rios, and Blaine Ludeman for your specific contributions to this publishing journey.

I am especially lucky to have old and new friends, colleagues, and family members who became an integral part of this project championing publication early on as well, including a community of individuals who contributed to my "Write to Heal and Thrive" GoFundMe publishing campaign. I appreciate each of you. To the many of you who have supported or shared your stories, Thank you! My life has been blessed with many kind and wonderful individuals and I hold you in my heart.

Next Steps

Thank you for journeying with me. Whether it is getting additional guidance or forming part of a support system for someone else, there are ways to use your voice and begin to thrive when you are ready to take additional steps. Forming and joining support groups, becoming a rape crisis center volunteer advocate in your community, and participating in marches and rallies to protest sexual violence are ways to connect with others who have had similar experiences. I sincerely hope my story will become a pivotal moment in someone's decision to actively start their healing process. By sharing this book with others who may benefit, or by writing a review on the platform you purchased it from, you become a spark to light another's healing flame.

It would be great to keep connecting via social media; Facebook, Instagram, and my website: *www.melissablombardo.com.* You may also use the hashtags **#hurthealinghopebook** and **#writehealthrive**

You may also contact me about media appearances, workshops, speaking at your events, assisting in producing Hurt, Healing, and Hope: Thriving beyond Sexual Assault at your school or in your community, or subscribing to my email list to learn more about my journey and upcoming publications.

Learn more at: *melissablombardo.com* or *writehealthrive.com*

Facebook: /Melissablombardoauthor

Instagram /Melissablombardoauthor

YouTube: /@MelissaBLombardoAuthor

DeafIGNITE.org. Supporting the needs of deaf survivors.

Endrapeoncampus.org. Works to end campus sexual violence.

EndSexualViolence.org. The National Alliance to End Sexual Violence.

Incestresourcesinc.org. All survivor, non-profit organization.

Invisiblegirlsthrive.com. Helping girls heal and move forward.

Joyfulheartfoundation.org. A national organization to transform society's response to sexual assault, domestic violence, and child abuse.

MaleSurvivor.org. Hope, healing, and support for male survivors.

Nomore.org. Dedicated to ending domestic violence and sexual assault through increasing awareness.

Transquality.org. National Center for Transgender Equality.

Ncadv.org. National Coalition Against Domestic Violence.

Nsvrc.org. The National Sexual Violence Resource Center.

Sidran.org. The Sidran Institute for Traumatic Stress, Education and Advocacy.

Takebackthenight.org. A worldwide movement and foundation standing against sexual violence.

Theclotheslineproject.org. National network of those affected by violence to express themselves.

Thehotline.org. National Domestic Violence hotline.

References

Burgess, A., & Holmstrom, L. (1979). *Rape: Crisis and recovery.* R. J. Brady Company.

Kennedy, D. M., & Hock, R. R. (2000). *It's my life now: Starting over after an abusive relationship or domestic violence.* Routledge Publishing.

Parrot, A. (1995). *Coping with date rape and acquaintance rape.* Rosen Publishing.

Rape Abuse and Incest National Network (R.A.I.N.N.). (n.d.). More statistics. Retrieved April 27, 2021, from *rainn.org/statistics*

Rape Abuse and Incest National Network (R.A.I.N.N.). (n.d.). Recovering from sexual violence. *rainn.org/recovering-sexual-violence*

Rape Abuse and Incest National Network (R.A.I.N.N.). (n.d.). Scope of problem: Statistics. Retrieved April 27, 2021, from *rainn.org/statistics/scope-problem*

Rape Abuse and Incest National Network (R.A.I.N.N.). (n.d.). Sexual assault. *rainn.org/articles/sexual-assault*

Rape Abuse and Incest National Network (R.A.I.N.N.). (n.d.). Victims of sexual violence: Statistics. Retrieved April 27, 2021, from *rainn.org/get-information/statistics/sexual-assault-victims*

Resilience. (n.d.). Effects of sexual violence. *ourresilience.org/what-you-need-to-know/effects-of-sexual-violence/*

Performance Notes

Use these following pages to write notes regarding your licensed performance to help you organize. You may include licensing information, contact information, budgeting, and any other notes that you might want to remember for later use.

If you would like assistance with production, please contact: *info@melissablombardo.com*

Performance Notes *(Continued)*

Performance Notes *(Continued)*

Meet Us

Photo credit:
Alicia Ann Daw
Stylist:
Jessica Dutton

Melissa Lombardo

Melissa Lombardo always had a passion for listening to and supporting those without a voice, which led her to travel throughout the United States, Europe, and Central America learning the experiences of others. Throughout her travels, she knew she needed to tell the stories she lived and heard from others, but she could not find the inner voice to speak. It was only after she made the decision to confront past trauma that she could move forward and thrive. Now, many years later she is determined to help others find their own voice and begin to actively heal. Melissa currently spends her time between her home state of Connecticut, U.S.A., and Nicaragua, the country of her heart.

Photo credit:
Eduardo José Arias Cruz

Eduardo José Arias Cruz

Eduardo José Arias Cruz, Nicaraguan visual artist, art instructor, and graphic designer brings the healing journey to life through these original watercolor illustrations. For more information about Eduardo, visit *eduardoariascruz.com*.

www.ingramcontent.com/pod-product-compliance
Lightning Source LLC
Chambersburg PA
CBHW051640120626
46551CB00014B/2156